To Boris and Rob
Mary Claire Smith

© Element Children's Books 1999
"little tree"
COMPLETE POEMS: 1904-1962
Copyright 1925, 1953, ©1991 by the Trustees for the E.E. Cummings Trust.
Copyright ©1976 by George James Firmage.
Illustrations © Mary Claire Smith 1999

First published in Great Britain in 1999 by
Element Children's Books
Shaftesbury, Dorset SP7 8BP

Published in the USA in 1999 by
Element Books, Inc.
160 North Washington Street,
Boston MA 02114

Published in Australia in 1999 by
Element Books and distributed by
Penguin Australia Limited,
487 Maroondah Highway, Ringwood,
Victoria 3134

Cover and text design by Mandy Sherliker.
Printed and bound in China

British Library Cataloguing in Publication data available.
Library of Congress Cataloging in Publication data available.

ISBN 1 902618 55 6

# little tree

## e.e. cummings

*Illustrated by Mary Claire Smith*

**ELEMENT**

**CHILDREN'S
BOOKS**

little tree
little silent Christmas tree

you are so little
you are more like a flower

who found you in the green forest
and were you very sorry to come away?

see        i will comfort you
because you smell so sweetly

i will kiss your cool bark
and hug you safe and tight
just as your mother would,
only don't be afraid

look        the spangles
that sleep all the year in a dark box
dreaming of being taken out and allowed to shine,
the balls the chains red and gold the fluffy threads,

put up your little arms
and i'll give them all to you to hold
every finger shall have its ring
and there won't be a single place dark or unhappy

then when you're quite dressed
you'll stand in the window for everyone to see
and how they'll stare!
oh but you'll be very proud

and my little sister and i will take hands
and looking up at our beautiful tree
we'll dance and sing

"Noel Noel"